Original title:
Inspiring Innovation

Copyright © 2024 Swan Charm Publishing
All rights reserved.

Editor: Jessica Elisabeth Luik
Author: Lan Donne
ISBN HARDBACK: 978-9916-86-318-3
ISBN PAPERBACK: 978-9916-86-543-9

Fractal Futures

In a realm where patterns weave,
Infinite loops that minds conceive,
Every turn unveils a clue,
Fractal visions, worlds anew.

Time revolves in cyclic streams,
Endless spirals chase our dreams,
Through the chaos, find the truth,
Echoes of eternal youth.

Universe in micro form,
Hidden depths within the storm,
Boundless paths our spirits trace,
Fractal futures interlace.

Out of the Blue

Sudden calm, the skies are still,
From the void, a gentle thrill,
Life emerges, colors blaze,
Out of the blue, a new phase.

Unexpected, wonders spring,
Like the song a bird might sing,
In the silence, whispers grew,
Out of the blue, dreams ensue.

Mysteries the world bestows,
In the heart, a spirit knows,
Through the fog, a clearer view,
Out of the blue, light breaks through.

The Symphony of Creation

In the silence before dawn,
Creation's whispers rise,
With each stroke of light,
A new world in our eyes.

From the chaos, order springs,
Stars in cosmic dance,
The universe in harmony,
A symphony of chance.

Nature's brush paints skies,
Coloring life anew,
Every sunset, a promise,
Of mornings to ensue.

Echoes of New Worlds

Through the void it travels,
A signal strong and sure,
From worlds beyond perception,
The echoes still endure.

Galaxies from afar,
Whispering ancient tales,
Mysteries of existence,
In celestial trails.

Time and space unravel,
On this voyage grand,
Discoveries unbounded,
In our cosmic hand.

Paradigms Shifted

When thoughts embrace the unknown,
Horizons start to bend,
The mind expands its realm,
Reality, transcend.

In the dance of ideas,
New visions come to light,
Old paradigms are shaken,
Till shadows become bright.

Knowledge ever-changing,
In this boundless stream,
Future paths enlightened,
By the power of a dream.

Embarking the Unexplored

Set sails into the vast,
Where maps no longer lead,
Dreams as our compass,
To worlds that we must heed.

From shores of the familiar,
To oceans deep and wide,
Charting the uncharted,
With stars to be our guide.

In the heart of mystery,
Courage finds its voice,
Embarking the unexplored,
Where earth and sky rejoice.

Fresh Perspectives

In shadows long, new light appears,
Emerging bright through foggy years.
Where old horizons fade away,
Fresh dreams arise to bloom and sway.

In silken threads of twilight's weave,
The dawn invites hearts to believe.
Whispers soft of future's call,
Fresh perspectives for one and all.

Through time's ever-shifting sands,
We hold new worlds within our hands.
Change is but a gentle breeze,
Fresh perspectives set minds at ease.

The Dawn of Genius

In quiet minds where thoughts entwine,
The seeds of brilliance start to shine.
From hidden depths, a spark ignites,
The dawn of genius takes its flight.

With whispered winds of insight's grace,
New visions form and interlace.
Through boundless night, ideas soar,
The dawn of genius opens the door.

In every question lies the key,
A curiosity set free.
From shadows dark, a guiding light,
The dawn of genius, pure and bright.

The Frontier of Thought

Beyond the veil of what we see,
Lies realms of endless mystery.
Exploring depths with eager hearts,
The frontier of thought never departs.

In every quest for what's unknown,
New pathways of the mind are sown.
With boundless courage, through the night,
The frontier of thought shines ever bright.

In ceaseless search for what could be,
Unveil the truths that set us free.
With every step, a world is caught,
Upon the vast frontier of thought.

Engineering Brilliance

In gears of time and waves of sound,
Engineering brilliance can be found.
With careful hands and minds so sharp,
They mold the world, create its arc.

From rivets strong to circuits bright,
Their visions stretch both day and night.
In every line and every spark,
Engineering brilliance leaves its mark.

They link the dreams to what is real,
With skills that shape and ideas that heal.
In every plan and every stance,
Engineering brilliance takes a chance.

Seeds of Imagination

Beneath the soil of thought,
Ideas quietly sprout,
In shadows cast by doubt,
A new dream is sought.

From whispers in the breeze,
They gather strength and grow,
Through winding paths unknown,
Toward skies of endless seas.

Each seed, a tiny spark,
Of possibilities vast,
Planted in landscapes vast,
In corners cool and dark.

Nurtured by hands unseen,
They pierce the crust of fear,
Reaching for light so near,
In gardens of the unseen.

Sparks of Creation

In the forge of the mind,
Flares of genius ignite,
Bright against the night,
A vision's form is lined.

Ideas meld and merge,
Fusion of thought and light,
Creativity's pure flight,
In an eternal surge.

Each spark a brand new dawn,
A possibility fresh,
Breaking from the mesh,
Of old conventions torn.

Creation's endless strive,
From chaos, order grows,
In boundless ebb and flows,
Where dreams are kept alive.

The Mind's Blueprints

In the realms of thought,
Plans and schemes reside,
Structures formed with pride,
In blueprints finely wrought.

Each line a testament,
To intellect and hope,
In webs of ideas cope,
Foundations firmament.

A map to future's gate,
Drawn by minds so clear,
Visions brought so near,
By drafts intricate.

Thus, reality is penned,
On sheets of mental space,
Every line a trace,
Of wisdom's steady blend.

Dreams into Reality

From slumber's soft embrace,
Visions take their flight,
In the still of night,
They find their sacred place.

Within the heart's deep core,
Dreams are crafted fine,
Boldly they align,
With aspirations' roar.

They wake to morning's glow,
Fleshed with form and grace,
In the daily race,
Their presence starts to show.

Reality is shaped,
By dreams once fragile streams,
Now solid as it seems,
In realms of effort draped.

The Genesis of Wonder

In the heart of night, stars send their gleam,
Whispering secrets, a celestial dream.
From void to cosmos, a spark ignites,
Born of darkness, the first dawn's light.

Mountains arose from deep ocean's chest,
Forests painted in hues of the best.
Life unfurled in a wondrous array,
Begin your tale, oh break of day.

Eyes open wide in innocent awe,
Nature's theater has no flaw.
Moments eternal, in silence profound,
Wonder's genesis, where marvels abound.

A Realm Beyond Boundaries

In fields where imagination flows,
Boundaries vanish, the spirit grows.
Castles of clouds in the azure sky,
Where dreams take flight, where fancies fly.

Beyond the visible, horizons extend,
A realm where realities blend.
Footsteps brave on paths untold,
Where visions of the heart unfold.

Time ceases ticking, space redefines,
In the theater of infinite signs.
Unseen dimensions, unfathomed deep,
Where mysteries of the cosmos sleep.

Crafting the Unconventional

With hands that shape what minds conceive,
In brilliance, the soul's reprieve.
From common clay, emerges the new,
Unbound by norms, dreams break through.

In shadows' dance and light's embrace,
Innovations wear a fearless face.
Undefined by the structured mind,
In chaos, beauty of its own kind.

Through unpaved paths, wanderers tread,
Bold creations where others dread.
Crafting the world from a curious gaze,
Unconventional art in the maker's craze.

The Future's Palette

On the canvas of tomorrow's dawn,
Colors of hope and dreams are drawn.
Brushstrokes of time in hues profound,
Visions emerge, where none confound.

In the sweep of possibility's arc,
New constellations in innovation spark.
Bound by not, the painter's streak,
Creating futures bold and sleek.

With every stroke, a world anew,
In shades of wonder, green and blue.
The palette of what yet shall be,
A masterpiece for all to see.

Blueprint to the Beyond

In cosmic dreams, a path unfolds,
Whispers of stars, a tale retold.
Beyond the veil, where secrets lie,
A map of hope against the sky.

Celestial ink on midnight hue,
Guiding hearts to worlds anew.
Constellations weave their thread,
Through twilight's dance where wishes spread.

Amidst the void, a light appears,
Charting a course through space's tears.
With every step, the darkness fades,
Revealing truths in stellar shades.

Eternal voyage through the night,
Seeking realms of endless light.
In every soul, the dream resides,
A blueprint drawn by cosmic tides.

The Dawn of Creation

From abyss dark, a spark ignites,
Birthing worlds from endless nights.
In the stillness, whispers grow,
Seeds of life begin to show.

Chaos yields to ordered rhyme,
Dancing through the dawn of time.
Stars from dust in radiant birth,
Crafting heavens, shaping Earth.

Rivers carved by ancient hands,
Mountains rise where silence stands.
Oceans deep with secrets sworn,
Life's first breath at break of morn.

Harmony in nature's scheme,
Unfolding like a timeless dream.
Every leaf, a tale it weaves,
In the dawn where fate believes.

The Forge of Ideas

Within the mind, a fire burns bright,
Lighting the path through endless night.
Sparks of thought in chaos play,
Forging visions in their sway.

Hammering dreams on anvils bold,
Shaping destinies untold.
Each idea, a crafted gem,
In the forge, we cherish them.

Through trial's flame, insights emerge,
Wisdom's depth where passions surge.
Boundless realms of innovation,
Born from fervent imagination.

Empires built on whispered themes,
Reality woven from our dreams.
In the forge of ideas, we find,
The essence of the boundless mind.

Sculpting the Future

With hands of hope, we shape the clay,
Molding dreams from night to day.
Each chisel marks a vision clear,
Crafting futures without fear.

From marble blocks of possibility,
We carve paths of tranquility.
Etching lines of progress grand,
Sketching what tomorrow's planned.

Traits of courage, strokes of light,
Sculpting change in endless fight.
Figures form with every touch,
In hands of hope, we trust so much.

Through patience, time reveals our view,
A future bright, a world anew.
In every heart, an artist thrives,
Sculpting futures with our lives.

Uncharted Pathways

Through forests deep and mountains high,
We wander where the eagles fly,
In search of dreams that never fade,
On pathways unmarked and unmade.

Underneath the starlit sky,
With hearts unbridled, we rely,
On hope's warm glow to light our way,
Through night and dawn, to break of day.

Oceans vast and deserts wide,
Through storm and calm, our spirits glide,
In quest of lands by none yet seen,
Crafting tales where none have been.

Horizons Unseen

Beneath the sun's first golden rise,
A world anew before our eyes,
Whispers of the winds unknown,
Call us to lands we've not yet shown.

Horizons stretch beyond the veils,
Of present fears and olden tales,
With every step on ground untold,
We journey forth, so brave and bold.

Twilight's veil and dawn's embrace,
Mark the timeless, endless chase,
For dreams that lie just out of sight,
Unseen horizons of pure light.

Seeds of Genius

In quiet moments, thoughts take flight,
Ideas bloom in silent night,
From seeds of wonder, genius grows,
Creating worlds only heart knows.

Whispers of imagination,
Crafted in sweet contemplation,
Each spark alights a vivid dream,
Setting minds on endless stream.

Branches stretch to skies unknown,
Bearing fruits of thought we've sown,
For in each seed, a galaxy,
Of endless creativity.

Beyond the Boundaries

Boundaries set by minds confined,
Shattered by the bold defined,
Venturing past the chains we know,
To places where new winds will blow.

Limitless, the vast expanse,
Invites our daring hearts to dance,
In realms where freedom finds its form,
And out of chaos, dreams are born.

With vision clear, we push ahead,
In unmarked lands where none have tread,
Where possibility is free,
And visions join in harmony.

Rise of New Worlds

In twilight's silent embrace, the dawn peeks,
Years whisper secrets in the brooks and creeks.
Unknown horizons call with colors bold,
A tapestry of tales yet to unfold.

Dreams awaken in the heart's quiet beat,
While shadows dance, the earth beneath our feet.
Stars wink softly from their cosmic heights,
Guiding us through dark and infinite nights.

With every step, we conquer fear's stronghold,
Mountains bow, their ancient stories told.
The winds of change usher in the dew,
For every night gives way to something new.

Symphonies of Tomorrow

Melodies weave through our tangled dreams,
Notes that shimmer in the moonlight's beams.
Whispers of futures yet unsung,
In every heart where hope is sprung.

Candles flicker in the shadowed hall,
Echoes of a time our spirits call.
In the thrum of life, the beat goes on,
Through dusk and dawn, dusk and dawn.

Rhythms merge in a transcendent sweep,
Crafting tales both loud and deep.
The symphony of tomorrow plays,
A testament to endless days.

Ventures Untold

On pages worn, ink begins to flow,
Stories of paths no one will know.
Brave hearts venture into the great unknown,
Journeying far from hearth and home.

Whispers of the wind guide their steps,
Leading where the sun never sets.
Discoveries bloom in the offbeat track,
In every corner, no turning back.

From mountaintops to valleys deep,
Secrets in whispers and silence keep.
Boldly they wander, these ventures untold,
In search of treasures worth more than gold.

Paths Uncharted

Where the moon's light meets the ancient trees,
We tread softly, whispers in the breeze.
Footsteps echo off the beaten roads,
Carrying dreams and untold loads.

In wildlands where the maps aren't drawn,
We find places reality's hands have never known.
Beyond the horizon, a quest unfolds,
In fields of silver and marigold.

With every step, courage blossoms bright,
Guiding souls through the unending night.
Paths uncharted, with secrets to reveal,
Marking trails that time cannot steal.

Pathways to Progress

In the heart of every trial,
A lantern's light will gleam,
Guiding through the darkest mile,
Fulfilling hopeful dreams.

Steps we take, though small arrayed,
Pave roads of grand design.
With courage, fear will soon be swayed,
And future brightly shine.

Mountains high and valleys low,
All challenge our intent.
Persistence makes the spirit grow,
In progress we relent.

Choices made from day to day,
Shape pathways yet unseen.
Our will and effort painting grey,
Into a vibrant scene.

Hand in hand, together strive,
In union, strength renew.
Pathways to progress we derive,
Through dreams that we pursue.

Evolution Through Imagination

Imagination spurs the soul,
To realms beyond our sight.
A spark within, a timeless role,
Transforming day to night.

Dreams unfurl their wings to fly,
Beyond the heights of air.
Painting visions in the sky,
New worlds beyond compare.

Through the canvas of the mind,
Creation takes its flight.
In the boundless thoughts, we find,
An everlasting light.

Innovation's gentle hand,
Crafts futures bold and bright.
With each imaginative strand,
We evolve in pure delight.

Journey inward, hearts explore,
Beyond the mere mundane.
Through imagination, open door,
Our spirits break the chain.

Windows to the Future

Gazing through the looking glass,
At times yet to unfold,
Visions of what will surpass,
Stories yet retold.

Windows to the future lie,
In dreams of yesterday.
Reflecting on the reasons why,
New paths await the fray.

Every choice, a window wide,
Opening to new dawns.
Through the panes our hopes confide,
Embracing futures drawn.

Possibilities abound,
In each reflective gaze.
Time's whispers as a subtle sound,
Guiding through life's maze.

In the frame, we place our trust,
To light the paths unseen.
Windows to the future thrust,
A journey yet serene.

Epiphanies Beckon

In moments still, the silence speaks,
Revelations near,
A whisper from the mountain peaks,
A truth so crystal clear.

Awareness blooms as morning dawn,
In rays of light and grace.
Epiphanies, old curtains drawn,
Their warmth we now embrace.

Hearts awaken to the sound,
Of wisdom gently stirred.
In the newfound joy, we're bound,
To echoes once unheard.

Each epiphany revealed,
A beacon in our night.
With light the path ahead is sealed,
And shadows take their flight.

Beckoning us to explore,
The depths of our own mind.
Epiphanies, through open door,
New understanding find.

The Art of the Possible

In dreams we sketch a boundless sky,
Colors blend as worlds collide.
From whispers turned to daring try,
In each attempt, new paths reside.

With courage lit, we dare create,
The unknown realms our spirits chase.
Through failures past and risks innate,
We sculpt a future, brave and vast.

An ember sparks within the mind,
No chains can hold what thoughts conceive.
A vision pure, untamed, aligned,
The art of hope, through dreams, achieved.

Beyond the Horizon

The sun dips low, a golden hue,
Where sea and sky in twilight blend.
It's there we glance, a world anew,
A place where dreams and hopes ascend.

Through shadows long, our footsteps lead,
Past mountains high and valleys deep.
Our spirits soar, hearts still and freed,
To realms where only courage leaps.

Beyond that line, where earth does end,
Lies mystery, wonder, endless bloom.
In reaching out, new paths extend,
And dreams ignite in twilight's loom.

Minds Unchained

Unbound by fear, our thoughts take flight,
Through realms untold, uncharted seas.
In darkness we ignite the light,
With wisdom's spark and daring please.

Shackles fall as minds expand,
Each chain a relic, rust and spite.
With open hearts and open hands,
We grasp at destiny, bold and bright.

In every challenge we perceive,
A chance to grow, transform, and learn.
Minds unchained, we break, believe,
And blaze a trail where ideas burn.

Renaissance of Ideas

From ashes rise the sparks of thought,
A rebirth of the mind's grand quest.
In quietude, in chaos caught,
Ideas bloom, in brilliance dressed.

The old gives way to visions clear,
Traditions bow to insights bold.
Within each mind, a new frontier,
A renaissance in truth unfolds.

Through ink and brush, through word and deed,
The seeds of wonder, sown and grown.
Imagination, knowledge freed,
In unity, a world reknown.

Creative Horizons

Beneath the sky where dreams take flight,
Imagination soars on wings of light.
Colors blend in a dance so free,
Crafting landscapes of possibility.

Voices whisper in the twilight's gleam,
Stories woven in a tapestry dream.
Ink flows like rivers on an open page,
Unveiling wonders stage by stage.

From dusk to dawn, the artist's hand,
Shapes the beauty, makes its stand.
Limits break, the mind unfurls,
A universe born, a world of pearls.

Songs of creation, melodies untold,
In the heart of silence, truths unfold.
Each stroke, each word a destined key,
Unlocks the vault of the soul's decree.

Embrace the unknown, let visions rise,
In the realm where magic never dies.
Dreams are seeds in the fertile soil,
Blooming with the essence of toil.

Visionary Pathways

Starlit roads where thoughts align,
Journeying through the realms divine.
Each step a promise, a spark so bright,
Guided by the radiant light.

Mountains whisper secrets old,
Pathways shimmer, stories told.
Eyes that see beyond the veils,
Crafting futures from ancient trails.

With every turn, a choice to make,
Determinations stir, foundations shake.
Dreamers tread where none have gone,
In their hearts, a destined dawn.

Wisdom carried on the breeze,
Softly spoken through the trees.
Pathways forged with heart and mind,
Seeking truths the lost may find.

In quest of stars, in search of dreams,
On visionary pathways, light redeems.
With courage bound and spirits high,
They've woven bridges to the sky.

Beyond the Ordinary

In realms where shadows fade away,
A world of marvels starts to sway.
Mysteries unfold, pure and grand,
Beyond the reach of common sand.

Whispers of the unknown call,
Through hidden doors in endless hall.
Adventures spark from embered skies,
Unlock the magic in disguise.

From everyday, a step aside,
Unveiling wonders where secrets hide.
Colors burst in vivid hues,
A canvas filled with countless views.

Beyond the ordinary, dreams unfurl,
Within this unseen, mystic whirl.
Moments cherished, timelessly,
In realms where life's extraordinary.

In fleeting glimpses, caught our gaze,
Through life's surreal, wondrous maze.
Beauty lies in sights unseen,
In places where imaginations glean.

Crafting the Future

Hands that mold tomorrow's clay,
Shaping dreams in light of day.
Vision turns to sturdy plan,
Brick by brick, in stride they stand.

Threads of time in fabric weave,
With every breath, beginnings breathe.
Hope engrained in hearts so bold,
Stories of the future told.

Craft the future with a spark,
In the daylight and the dark.
One by one, paths form anew,
Guided by the dreamer's view.

Possibilities, endless streams,
Flow within, unclaimed dreams.
Minds create, with fervor bright,
Destinies unfold in light.

Together forging what will be,
In unity, with harmony.
Bright horizons, crafted pure,
A future built, forever sure.

Unveil the Unseen

Beneath the veil of night, dreams take flight,
Whispers of hope in the quiet moonlight.
Wonders unseen, in shadows reside,
A world within, where mysteries hide.

Stars tell tales of ages gone by,
In silent twinkles that light up the sky.
Unfamiliar truths in darkness grow,
Revealing worlds we scarcely know.

Wisps of thoughts in twilight's embrace,
Guide us gently to a hidden space.
Beyond the obvious, secrets lie,
In the crevices of a questioning eye.

Glimpses of what could be, and once was,
Echoes of time in a silent pause.
So let imagination cast its gleam,
To unveil the depths of the unseen dream.

Through the layers of perception, we may find,
The beauty hidden in the quiet mind.
Unveil the unseen, let curiosity rise,
Exploring the realms behind closed eyes.

The Genesis of Ideas

In the stillness of the early morn,
Where silence reigns, ideas are born.
From the whispers of a waking mind,
New concepts and dreams, we hope to find.

A spark ignites in the quietest hour,
A thought blooms like a delicate flower.
From nothingness, something grows,
An idea forms as inspiration flows.

In the confluence of chaos and calm,
Ideas rise like a soothing psalm.
With each new dawn, a seed is sown,
In the fertile ground of the unknown.

In the tapestry of the unseen,
Colors of thought vibrant and keen.
Each idea, a painter's brush,
Crafting visions in a creative hush.

From the void, a universe springs,
A symphony of imagined things.
In the genesis of ideas, we find,
The endless wonders of our mind.

Boundless Conceptions

Imagination's boundless flight,
Soars beyond the darkest night.
Dreams untamed in endless skies,
A kaleidoscope before our eyes.

Infinite realms of thought and lore,
Await discovery evermore.
Boundless conceptions, visions grand,
Stories sculpted by unseen hands.

In the depths of a creative sea,
Lies a world of pure fantasy.
Each idea, a brand-new dawn,
Shaping realities yet to be drawn.

Through the corridors of the mind,
Ideas and dreams we start to find.
Uncharted lands and distant stars,
Imagination breaks all bars.

In the heart of dreams, we trust,
Boundless conceptions rise from dust.
A universe crafted from the unseen,
Where possibility reigns supreme.

The Loom of Progress

Threads of vision interlace,
In the loom, our dreams we trace.
Progress weaves through time and space,
Crafting futures we embrace.

With every thread, a story told,
A tapestry of brave and bold.
In each pattern, hope unfolds,
A vision for an era gold.

Through trials met and tests endured,
Progress shines, a path assured.
In the loom of effort pure,
The fabric strong, our dreams secure.

Innovation's gentle hand,
Guides the loom across the land.
With each thread, we understand,
The future's built where dreams expand.

In the weave of thought and deed,
Progress plants a hopeful seed.
An endless journey, minds freed,
In the loom of progress, lives lead.

Alchemy of Thought

In the shadows of the mind,
A subtle magic weaves its art,
Transforming whispers into gold,
The alchemy of thought, a start.

Mysterious as the night so deep,
Dreams take flight on alchemical wings,
From leaden fears, new hope we reap,
In every thought, creation springs.

Ideas flicker, sparks ignite,
Crafting worlds unseen, so grand,
Through the mind's kaleidoscope,
We shape the stars with steady hand.

Philosopher's stones of intellect,
Turn mundane to sublime,
In the lab of consciousness,
We transcend both space and time.

The furnace of the inward eye,
Melts down worries, forging new,
Through thought's alchemy, we fly,
Transforming old in every view.

Future's Fabric

Threads of fate, both bright and stark,
Woven in the loom of time,
Future's fabric, dark and light,
Sings an endless rhyme.

Patterns shifting, merging hues,
Pathways that our hearts may choose,
In the tapestry unfurled,
Dreams and destinies diffuse.

A needle's point of hope and fear,
Stitches lives both far and near,
In each weave, a story told,
Of past, of present, futures clear.

Colors blend, a dance of days,
In the warp and weft we lay,
Future's fabric, vast and free,
Guiding us upon our way.

Every thread, a chance anew,
In the loom of life we view,
We weave our tales with care and grace,
Each line a glimpse of places true.

The Next Dimension

Beyond the realms of sight and sound,
A world awaits, profound, unseen,
Where whispers of the cosmos speak,
In patterns vast and crystalline.

A journey through the void we start,
Across the planes where shadows blend,
Dimensions fold within our minds,
In endless loops, they twist and bend.

Luminous the paths we tread,
Stars align to light our way,
Through portals vast and windows small,
We glimpse the birth of another day.

In the sphere of thought and dream,
New dimensions lie ahead,
Reality is but a seam,
Between the living and the dead.

Explorers of the next frontier,
With hearts as maps, and minds as sails,
We transcend the world's veneer,
And unlock the universe's tales.

Thought Alchemy

Through synaptic fire, we conjure light,
From darkest depths, new hope we glean,
Transmuting sorrow into bright,
Thoughts alchemize to dreams unseen.

Mysteries of the heart and soul,
In reason's forge are purified,
Alchemy of mind makes whole,
What life's enigmas often hide.

With every spark of inner flame,
Ideas like meteors do ignite,
We chase the shadows, and proclaim,
Spectrum's glory by thought's light.

In the crucible of intent,
Whispers turn to thunder's roar,
Alchemy of thought invents,
Realms of wonder to explore.

From grief's leaden, heavy chain,
To joy's gold, so brightly sought,
We craft anew, within the brain,
The alchemy that is deep thought.

Catalysts of Change

In the stillness of night, whispers arose,
Carried by breezes, where the moonlight flows.
Each word a spark, igniting our soul,
Change in the air, making us whole.

Seeds of tomorrow, in the present we sow,
Waters of hope help them to grow.
From darkness to dawn, the colors arrange,
We stand as one, catalysts of change.

Mountains were moved and rivers redefined,
Courage in heart and peace in the mind.
With each small act, the world rearranged,
We became the catalysts of change.

Threads of the future, weaving our fate,
Bound by compassion, stronger than hate.
Hand in hand, horizons estrange,
Together, we'll be catalysts of change.

Voices united, breaking the cage,
Birthed from the storms, a brand new age.
Purpose renewed, destinies exchange,
Forever, we'll be catalysts of change.

Awakening Ideas

From the depths of silence, whispers grew,
Thoughts intertwined, both brilliant and true.
In the mind's eye, new worlds appear,
Awakening ideas, breaking fear.

Every moment, a canvas pristine,
Imagination's brush, vivid and keen.
Dreams woven tightly, no boundary it heeds,
Awakening ideas, planting seeds.

A spark of genius in the heart's core,
Unveiling wonders never seen before.
Silent echoes scream, innovation leads,
Awakening ideas, fulfilling needs.

The dawn of thought, in twilight gleams,
Reality blends with boundless dreams.
In the quiet corners, inspiration feeds,
Awakening ideas, broader deeds.

Through Time's vast labyrinth, echoes play,
Guiding the lost by night and day.
Endless horizons, existence exceeds,
Awakening ideas, timeless creeds.

The Spark Within

In every heart, a secret lies,
A flicker of light that never dies.
Hidden beneath the scars so thin,
Waiting to ignite, the spark within.

Through trials faced and battles won,
The healing begins when the day is done.
Strength emerges where shadows had been,
Embracing the warmth of the spark within.

Hope rekindled in moments of strife,
Guides us through the labyrinth of life.
In quiet whispers, answers akin,
Trusting the glow of the spark within.

Mountains we climb, rivers we cross,
Learning to cherish, learning of loss.
With every step and where we've been,
Ever brighter shines the spark within.

In unity, our spirits align,
The fire inside begins to shine.
Together we'll rise, the dance will begin,
Fueled by the timeless spark within.

Visionary Dreams

Beyond the veil of sleep, they soar,
Visions that beckon evermore.
Silent whispers of what could be,
Visionary dreams, wild and free.

The canvas of night, stars painting bright,
Scenes of tomorrow in the soft light.
Guiding our paths, though futures seem,
Shaped by the glow of visionary dreams.

In realms unseen, they scatter gold,
Stories of future waiting to be told.
Fueled by passions, unbound streams,
Crafted by endless visionary dreams.

Oceans of hope beneath twilight's hush,
Carry our souls in a gentle rush.
To places unknown, with radiant beams,
We traverse the waves of visionary dreams.

When dawn breaks through, a new day warms,
Born from the night amidst life's storms.
Reality forms from moonlit seams,
Waking the world with visionary dreams.

Future Blueprint

In a world sketched in silver light,
Dreams weave through the dark of night.
Blueprints drawn with stars aglow,
Whispers of where futures grow.

Pages turned with hope's own hand,
Plans unfurl in twilight's land.
Timeless visions softly appear,
Crafting tomorrows, crystal clear.

Sweeping arcs of destiny,
Born from pure serendipity.
Echoes of a silent call,
Answering dreams that will enthrall.

Infinite paths of cosmic dust,
Lodestars for hearts to trust.
Figures in the endless scope,
Mapping the journey with hope.

Imprints of tomorrow's grace,
Traced in every secret place.
Celestial guides in shadows cast,
Future's light, a beacon vast.

Enigmatic Sparks

In a realm of darkened light,
Shadows dance, taking flight.
Sparks ignite the unseen plain,
Mysteries whispered in the rain.

Each spark a tale, unknown, unsaid,
Illuminating paths we tread.
In the void where echoes sing,
Secrets born in every ring.

Cryptic symbols in the night,
Lit by sparks, so fierce, so bright.
Whispers weave in silent streams,
Where reality begets dreams.

Hidden flames ignite the soul,
In the night, shadows unroll.
Mystic fires, eternal quest,
Burning questions never rest.

In the heart's enigma, stark,
Lie the seeds of every spark.
As sparks dance and shadows weave,
Truths emerge for those who believe.

The Dream Architect

Architect of dreams, so fine,
Builds in realms where wishes dine.
Crafting towers in the blue,
Designs born of thoughts anew.

Blueprints scrawled on twilight's veil,
Dreams embarked on starlit trail.
Foundations firm on whispered breeze,
Structures rise with graceful ease.

Casting shadows tall and grand,
In a world by vision's hand.
Painters of ethereal hues,
Weave through nights of silken blues.

From the depths of boundless thought,
Infinite designs are wrought.
In each dream, an artist's mark,
A gleaming flame within the dark.

As morning dawns with gilded hue,
Dreamscapes fade, yet hold their due.
Guardian of visions dear,
The Dream Architect draws near.

Fusion of Thoughts

Minds converge in silent streams,
Flowing worlds of endless dreams.
Fusion of thoughts, a cosmic dance,
Whispers caught in fates' expanse.

Ideas blend in twilight's glow,
Waves of wonder ebb and flow.
Curved in arcs of boundless reach,
Truths and mysteries softly teach.

Threads of thought entwine in grace,
Weaving realms in boundless space.
Each conception sparks anew,
Insight traced in every hue.

Synapses spark, a bridge of light,
Across the voids of endless night.
Visions meld to craft the stream,
Fusion born from silent dream.

In the confluence, so grand,
Wisdom guides with gentle hand.
Fusion of thoughts, a radiant shore,
Minds united evermore.

The Pulse of Pioneers

In fields of silent, golden grain,
Where dreams are sown, and hope remains,
Pioneers tread with vision clear,
Their whispers loud, we lend an ear.

With calloused hands and hearts agleam,
They sculpted life from versed dream,
Through storms and stars and cosmic ties,
They forged their fate, celestial skies.

Each step a cadence, firm and sure,
In shadows cast where light demurs,
They pressed forth, a trail they made,
Their legacy a bright cascade.

The echoes of their bold traverse,
Their spirits in the universe,
In pathways new, they chart and guide,
The pulse of pioneers, worldwide.

Among the heavens, earth and sea,
Their strides echo eternally,
For future souls to seek and find,
The pulse of pioneers, entwined.

The DNA of Discovery

In strands of light, the codes entwine,
Unraveling secrets, threads divine,
Through helix twists and paths unknown,
Discovery's seed is ever sown.

Cosmic patterns, mysteries vast,
To understand the future cast,
In labs aglow with thoughts unveiled,
The DNA of truth prevails.

Each molecule a puzzle piece,
A journey where explorations cease,
Within the silent, smallest part,
Discovery ignites the heart.

From ancient stars to newest life,
It navigates through endless strife,
In every spark, in every cell,
The quest for knowledge, tales to tell.

The pulse of time, a rhythm grand,
In every breakthrough, every strand,
The essence pure of what could be,
We honor in discovery's key.

Frontiers of Thought

Upon the edge of reason's light,
Where shadows dance within the night,
New realms of mind come into view,
Frontiers of thought, profound and true.

A voyage through the abstract seas,
Where questions flow like autumn leaves,
Beyond the known, beyond the seen,
To realms where only dreams convene.

Ideas spark like stars anew,
Through constellations bold and true,
Explorers of the thinking realm,
In cognitive ships, they steer and helm.

With every leap, with every find,
We inch towards the grand design,
The universe within our sight,
Ignites a future burning bright.

Through webs of knowledge, tightly spun,
Our journey's thread has just begun,
For in the halls where thoughts reside,
Immortal, boundless, free they glide.

Luminous Endeavors

Through shadows cast and darkness deep,
Where unknown truths in silence sleep,
The flame of mind illuminates,
In quests where brilliance orchestrates.

Embarking on ambitious trails,
Where courage reigns and doubt derails,
Pioneers of luminous dreams,
Unveil the stars in cosmic beams.

Their pathways carved in light profound,
Where every challenge, every bound,
Yields wonders bright, discoveries fair,
A testament of how we dare.

Each step they take defies the night,
In every spark, in every light,
We see the echoes of their strife,
Their luminous endeavors, life.

Through time and space, their spirits soar,
In endless quests for ever more,
Pursuits unending, bold, and pure,
Their luminous endeavors endure.

Embers of Transformation

In twilight's grasp, the embers glow,
Silent whispers of change bestow.
Old scars heal, new paths unfurl,
Within the night, dreams softly twirl.

Through ashes gray, life's fluid art,
Molds a future from each heart.
Hope rekindles, fears recede,
Light emerges from the need.

Winds of change in gentle sway,
Guide us toward the breaking day.
Past and present intertwine,
Forging futures, pure, divine.

From ember's spark, a fire ignites,
Blazing truths through endless nights.
Transformation's timeless dance,
Core of life's steadfast romance.

Resilient spirits, bold and free,
Embrace the endless, boundless sea.
In every heart, a ember's light,
Guides each soul through darkest night.

Navigating New Realms

Through uncharted seas we sail,
Beneath the skies both bright and pale.
Unknown worlds on horizons wide,
Invite our hearts to coincide.

Stars align with cosmic grace,
Guiding us through time and space.
Each new realm a story told,
In whispers soft and secrets bold.

Alien moons, with silver sheen,
Guard the pathways, yet unseen.
Mysteries in shadows lie,
Within the light, the truth will fly.

Navigating through the tides,
Unified, our spirits glide.
Bound by dreams, unchained by fear,
Every challenge brings us near.

As we journey, realms unfold,
In each adventure, truths untold.
Boundless realms through night and sun,
Each new quest, a world begun.

The Craft of Tomorrow

In workshops bright with future's gleam,
Craftsmen shape a vibrant dream.
Wonders born from hands precise,
Crafting futures, bold and nice.

Blueprints drawn from visions vast,
Guide the work, which shadows cast.
Fine-tuned skills in unity,
Forge the realm of what will be.

Machines hum with mindful care,
Weaving futures in the air.
Innovation lights the path,
Breaking molds in fresh aftermath.

Through each trial, persistence thrives,
As human spirit redefines.
Crafted futures, bold and high,
Rise to meet the dreaming sky.

In the craftsman's steady hand,
Lies the hope for every land.
Future's shape within our grasp,
Craft of tomorrow, firm and fast.

Breakthrough Odyssey

In the depths of endless night,
Breakthrough journeys seek the light.
Bold explorers, hearts awake,
Charted ways, and paths to break.

Through the storms and skies above,
Driven by a quest for love.
Every trial a compass shows,
Towards the dawn where beauty grows.

Unseen lands and new frontiers,
Conquered through both hope and tears.
Every step a mark of grace,
In this fateful, daring chase.

Odyssey of heart and mind,
Leaves the fearing past behind.
Boundless courage, firm and bright,
Navigates through darkest night.

Triumph calls through endless spree,
Of those who quest for destiny.
In the heart of every quest,
Lie breakthroughs where dreams rest.

Inventive Wings

In the realm where dreams take flight,
Soaring high in boundless skies.
Luminous stars guide the night,
In this world, we rise, we rise.

Echoes of a distant call,
Whispers of a future bright.
Building wonders, breaking walls,
Crafting visions in our sight.

Imagination takes its course,
Inventive wings of sheer delight.
Strengthened by a hidden force,
Leading us to bold new heights.

Fear not the unknown abyss,
For therein lies our inner might.
In every failure, newfound bliss,
We learn to navigate the night.

Creation born from mere belief,
Carried by our daring flight.
With inventive wings of relief,
We transcend the endless night.

Pioneering Spirit

Braving paths untrod before,
Hearts ablaze with fearless fire.
Charting routes to distant shores,
Driven by a deep desire.

In the wild, the unknown calls,
Whispering secrets, journeys new.
Breaking free from ancient thralls,
We seek worlds of every hue.

The spirit of the pioneer,
Unyielding in its mighty quest.
With every step, the world is clear,
We find ourselves and all the rest.

Challenges we'll face head-on,
Fueled by courage, inner light.
In the dawn, our dreams are drawn,
Guiding us through darkest night.

To innovate, to craft, to build,
A future bright, a hopeful cheer.
With pioneering hearts instilled,
We blaze the trail, we conquer fear.

Boundless Thinking

In the realm of endless thought,
Minds unfurl like blooming flowers.
Every idea, every plot,
Turns minutes into thinking hours.

No limits to the vast expanse,
Where creativity takes flight.
Each new vision, a daring dance,
Illuminates the darkest night.

From the well of endless dreams,
Insights pour like summer rain.
In between the layered seams,
Lies the key to break the chain.

Boundless minds explore the sky,
Bridging gaps that once were wide.
With each question, wonders fly,
Guided by an inner tide.

Untethered minds, forever free,
Crafting futures, bright and new.
Boundless thinking holds the key,
To worlds beyond, to what is true.

A Symphony of Ideas

In the concert of the mind,
Harmony of thoughts prevail.
Every note, a vision clear,
Within, the heart of ideas sails.

Melodies of dreams unite,
Crafting sounds of pure delight.
Inspiration in the night,
Guided by creative light.

Every concept forms a chord,
Resonating deep within.
In this symphony, we're floored,
New beginnings do begin.

Echoes of a future seen,
In the blend of thoughts and dreams.
Crafting realms of evergreen,
Where the boundless spirit gleams.

Ideas rise like morning's sun,
Each a spark in endless seas.
In this symphony, we're one,
Creating timeless legacies.

Exploring Possibilities

Beneath the endless azure skies,
Our spirits seek where dreams arise.
In fields of thought, where limits cease,
We chase the winds of wild surmise.

Through canyons deep and mountains high,
We scale the walls where shadows lie.
With hearts unchained by earthly ties,
Exploring paths where eagles fly.

Beyond the stars, past doubts' disguise,
We chart a course through cosmic size.
In realms unknown, with clear, bright eyes,
We find the truths that seem so wise.

Each step ahead, an untold tale,
In lands where whispered secrets sail.
Our journey's end, the final grail,
Is written where the dreamers dwell.

To maps unmade, to places rare,
We venture forth without a care.
In endless quests, we claim our share,
Of all the wonders waiting there.

The Canvas of Tomorrow

A blank expanse, the future bright,
Awaits the colors of our sight.
With every stroke, the dreams take flight,
On canvas pure as morning light.

With brush in hand, hope's hues we blend,
Creating scenes that never end.
In every shade, new worlds we send,
To futures that our hearts transcend.

Each pigment tells a story true,
Of visions fresh and skies so blue.
In twilight's glow, the mysteries brew,
As galaxies in paint renew.

The dawn of days yet born we see,
In strokes of possibility.
The canvas of tomorrow free,
To be the masterpiece we plea.

Where thoughts and wishes intertwine,
In frames of time, they glimmer, shine.
A symphony of dreams divine,
Unfolding on a grand design.

Architects of Tomorrow

With minds as sharp as finest steel,
We craft the dreams that worlds reveal.
In blueprints bold and visions real,
We build the futures we can feel.

Our hands, they mold in shapes so true,
The structures grand, the skies so new.
With every brick, the hope accrues,
As towers rise in morning dew.

From dreams to stone, the plans we lay,
In towering arcs of light and clay.
Through night and dawn, in dusk and day,
We pave the paths of future's way.

In cities bright with thoughts that breathe,
We weave the dreams the hearts bequeath.
In every spire, the spirits wreath,
A testament to what we seek.

With every line and every rhyme,
We etch the stories into time.
As architects, in heights we climb,
Creating realms where visions chime.

Idea Alchemists

In realms where thoughts like rivers flow,
We stir the depths where ideas grow.
As alchemists of mind's great glow,
We weave the gold from dawn's soft show.

With words like scrolls on winds we cast,
We shape the future from the past.
In whispers bright, the spells we grasp,
To turn the dreams to truths that last.

Through storm and calm, in night and day,
We craft the worlds our minds portray.
With every spark, a guiding ray,
Of alchemies that light the way.

From shadows deep and endless night,
We forge the beams of endless light.
In cauldrons vast, the dreams ignite,
Transforming thoughts with pure delight.

As sorcerers of realms unseen,
We conjure wonders yet to glean.
In every thought, a hidden sheen,
Of magic pure, and evergreen.

Catalysts of Change

In the depths of calm, a spark does birth,
Tiny flecks in quiet night,
A beating pulse beneath the earth,
Fanning dreams to boundless height.

Hands of time, in gentle waves,
Erode the old, reveal the new,
Silent echoes in hidden caves,
Carve pathways toward the view.

Whispers of the winds do speak,
Of fires that once burned low,
Now igniting peaks so bleak,
In a radiant, golden glow.

Roots of old, in fertile soil,
Yield the blossoms, fresh embrace,
Turning with the endless toil,
Makers of another place.

Boldly step where others fear,
In the shadows, light is found,
Catalysts of change are near,
In transformations, we are bound.

Visionary Currents

Currents flow through time and space,
Washing doubts and fears away,
Every wave, a new embrace,
Guiding us to break of day.

Mystic visions in the haze,
Pierce the veils of what could be,
Dreams that dance in varied ways,
On the winds, they venture free.

Ripples from the ancient streams,
Sketch a world that yet unfolds,
Mapping out our bravest dreams,
In patterns, bright and bold.

Through the mists of what is known,
Lies the path ahead, uncharted,
With each step, new seeds are sown,
Future hues, multi-hearted.

Raise your sails, embrace the flow,
Visionary winds shall guide,
In the currents, wisdom grows,
Voyagers of the shifting tides.

Mapping the Unseen

Wanderers on a journey deep,
Through terrains of shadowed thought,
In the vastness, secrets keep,
Contours by the stars are wrought.

Silent roads through midnight skies,
Pathways hidden from plain sight,
Mapping out where mystery lies,
Charting realms in the night.

Whispers from the ancient lore,
Guides of old direct the way,
In the unseen, there's so much more,
Than in the light of day.

Steps we take in quiet dusk,
Reveal truths we cannot deem,
In the cloak of twilight's husk,
We map realms within the dream.

Evermore, the quest proceeds,
Mapping unseen's endless flight,
In the dark, our mind exceeds,
Boundaries of the day's bright light.

A Universe of Thought

In the mind, a universe spins,
Galaxies of wondrous light,
Thoughts like stars, where dawn begins,
Scattering brilliance through the night.

Nebulas of dreams unfurled,
Spiral through the endless skies,
In the mind's expansive world,
Ideas like constellations rise.

Comets blaze through realms unknown,
Traces of creative flare,
Unseen worlds, by thoughts alone,
Reveal wonders floating there.

In the vastness of the brain,
Cosmos merge, collide, create,
Threads of logic, like a chain,
Bind the vast, explore the great.

A universe within us lies,
Endless in its boundless plot,
Journey through where wisdom flies,
In the universe of thought.

Crafting Potential

In the quiet of a humble room,
Ideas unfurl like petals in bloom.
Hands weave dreams with gentle care,
Crafting potential in the still air.

From raw thought to tangible form,
Imagination's spark keeps warm.
A world of wonders, unmade and free,
Awaits the art of discovery.

In silence, creation whispers loud,
Turning visions into the proud.
Each brushstroke, every hue,
Shapes a future bright and new.

Boundless realms in crafted mold,
As stories of tomorrow unfold.
Embrace the spark, let it shine,
Crafting potential, yours and mine.

The Landscape of Ingenuity

Across the hills where ideas roam,
Fields of thought, a fertile loam.
Mountains tall of daring schemes,
Rivers flow with endless dreams.

Innovation's wind through forests sweep,
Whispers secrets, deep in sleep.
Grasslands stretch to horizon's end,
Where creativity knows no bend.

In valleys carved by curious hands,
Wisdom's seed in fertile lands.
A landscape rich with countless hues,
Each one a spark of something new.

Bridges span through realms untold,
Connecting old with the bold.
In this land of endless quest,
Imagination finds its rest.

With every step, a new discovery,
In the landscape of ingenuity.
A boundless canvas, sky to sea,
Where dreams become reality.

The Muse's Laboratory

Where midnight oil and stardust mix,
The Muse conducts her clever tricks.
Beakers bubble with potential bright,
In her lab, beneath the night.

Ideas ignite, like lightning's spark,
Within her mind, creations arc.
Through trial, error, and delight,
She molds the dark into the light.

Sketches, drafts, and bold designs,
Blueprints of the grandest kinds.
Each experiment, a quest anew,
In search of something tried and true.

Shelves of thought in perfect rows,
Where inspiration freely flows.
The Muse's hand, so deft and skilled,
With every notion, heart is thrilled.

In her lab, the future swells,
With whispered dreams and chiming bells.
The Muse's touch in every part,
Creating wonders from the heart.

Bold New World

A dawn breaks on a world anew,
Where skies stretch wide, forever blue.
Possibilities in every fold,
A canvas bright, a story told.

Steps unmarked by paths before,
To explore and to adore.
Innovation's hand in tender care,
Crafts a future, bright and rare.

Through fields of thought, we venture far,
Guided by curiosity's star.
Mountains climb, yet spirits high,
In bold new world, we reach the sky.

Unbound by chains of yesteryears,
We pursue what hope endears.
With courage, strength, and boundless zeal,
We shape a world where dreams are real.

With every breath, a challenge met,
In this world, there's no regret.
Together, hand in hand we stride,
In bold new world, forever tied.

Nova Insights

In starry depths, the wisdom lies,
A beacon through the dark night skies.
Cosmic secrets start to rise,
Revealed to searching, eager eyes.

Galaxies in radiant spin,
Whisper tales of where we've been.
Each nova born, where dreams begin,
Invites us in, a cosmic kin.

Patterns form within the light,
Guiding souls through endless night.
In every spark, a hopeful sight,
A journey to the stars' delight.

Wisdom etched in stellar glow,
Each new insight helps us grow.
Though vast the space, we still know,
The path ahead is what we sow.

Gentle whispers, cosmic streams,
Filling voids with lucid dreams.
In the vastness, light redeems,
Shining through celestial themes.

Eclipsing the Mundane

In lives of gray, a sudden spark,
Something hidden, bright and stark.
Eclipsing shadows, leaving mark,
Transforming night into an arc.

Ordinary fades away,
Colors burst in rich array.
Moments weave a brighter day,
In magic's grasp, we freely play.

Eclipsing dull with vivid hues,
We break the chains, we choose our views.
Life once plain now to amuse,
Each moment fresh, like morning dews.

Casting off the cloak of bland,
Feet now dance on golden sand.
In the rare, we choose to stand,
Clutching dreams within our hand.

Transcend the ordinary scheme,
Riding waves of newfound gleam.
In the extraordinary stream,
We float through life, a waking dream.

Infinite Possibilities

Horizons broad, no end in sight,
A world of endless, pure delight.
Every dawn brings latent might,
Infinite paths to reach the light.

Dreams unfurl in star-kissed skies,
Hope renews as old fear dies.
Each step taken, new surprise,
Paths untraveled, we devise.

In the vast, no bounds confine,
Every soul with stars align.
In the possible, we shine,
Infinite futures intertwine.

Whispers gentle, softly speak,
Infinite journeys we can seek.
Future calls in vibrant streak,
Strength within, never meek.

Endless cycles, ripe for try,
Infinite, we soar and fly.
Possibilities amplify,
Together, dreams will clarify.

The Birth of Brilliance

In the dark, a spark ignites,
Tiny glow dispels the nights.
From the void, a new flame fights,
Birthing brilliance, stars in sight.

Seeds of light in fertile ground,
Spreading warmth, a glow unbound.
Silent whispers grow to sound,
Ideas take their first surround.

With each spark, the darkness fades,
Brilliance blossoms in soft shades.
Casting light through endless glades,
Guiding wanderers through life's mazes.

Hope is born where light abounds,
In each heart, a joy resounds.
Brilliance flourishes, knows no bounds,
Spreading warmth in endless rounds.

Morning comes, the dawn is bright,
Brilliance dances in the light.
In its glow, we find our might,
New beginnings, spirits height.

Surging Beyond Limits

In the shadow of the mountains tall,
We hear a whispering, gentle call,
A surge of power breaks the night,
Guiding us to newfound heights.

Beneath the stars, ambitions rise,
Dreams ride on the moonlit skies,
Boundaries fade, and we feel the thrill,
Riding waves of boundless will.

Courage blazes in our veins,
Relentless as the pouring rains,
Beyond the horizon, futures gleam,
A testament to every dream.

No chains can hold, no walls confine,
Driven by a force divine,
Beyond the limits, spirits soar,
Unleashing strength from every core.

Through valleys deep and oceans wide,
Together, we shall turn the tide,
Boundless hearts and minds, we strive,
In unity, our dreams revive.

Horizons of Creation

On the canvas of a morning spread,
With hues of hope in gold and red,
Imagination takes its flight,
Crafting worlds in endless light.

From the depths of thought it springs,
Where inspiration's music sings,
Wonders from the shadows brought,
Boundless realms of endless thought.

In each moment, pure and bright,
Lives the spark of pure delight,
Bridging dreams from heart to heart,
In this boundless work of art.

Infinite the paths we trace,
In the cosmic web of space,
As starlit dreams in twilight's court,
Unveil the realms where dreams comport.

Hand in hand, we shape our fate,
On the shores where dawn elates,
We sculpt the future's vivid sway,
In the dawn of each new day.

Pioneers of the New Dawn

On the threshold, dawn arrives,
With a promise that revives,
A legion of the bold and brave,
Marching forth, the world to save.

With eyes that gleam with future's light,
And hearts imbued with boundless might,
We forge our path through untamed lands,
With dreams as guides, and hope in hand.

Each step we take, a mark we leave,
In the tapestry we weave,
With courage fierce, and vision clear,
A legacy for those who're near.

Beyond the clouds, horizons call,
With echoes of a brighter hall,
We are the pioneers of today,
Carving out a brand-new way.

Together, we ignite the flame,
Of progress in the human name,
Lighting paths that stretch afar,
Guided by our guiding star.

Beyond Today

In the quiet of the twilight hour,
Whispers of a secret power,
Echoes of a time yet born,
Promise of a bright new morn.

Today we stand upon the crest,
Of mountains we have faced and best,
With hearts prepared, we look ahead,
To future paths where we are led.

Through each challenge that we face,
We'll navigate with strength and grace,
Eyes fixed beyond the here and now,
With dreams that guide us, like a vow.

Every moment, every choice,
Lends power to our inner voice,
In the tapestry of days, we weave,
A legacy we'll not reprieve.

Beyond today, beyond the strife,
We reach for more, we embrace life,
With hope as guide, and love as key,
We craft the future, bold and free.

A Tapestry of Discovery

In the quiet dawn of morning light,
New paths unfold, mysteries ignite,
Threads of wonder weave the air,
Adventure whispers everywhere.

Through tangled woods and rivers wide,
Curiosity becomes our guide,
Each step a journey, each sight a clue,
Worlds unseen come into view.

Stars above and roots beneath,
Echo stories that time bequeaths,
We tread the line 'tween known and new,
Embrace the magic of what we pursue.

With open heart and eager mind,
The quest for truth in all we find,
From deepest ocean to highest tree,
A tapestry of discovery.

As sun sets on another day,
New questions bloom and shadows play,
Until the morn with eager eyes,
We'll chase the dreams that light our skies.

Visionary Architects

With hands that dream and eyes that see,
Blueprints of possibility,
Foundations strong, ideas vast,
We build the future from the past.

Skyward towers, bridges grand,
Structures born from mind to hand,
In every beam and every stone,
The heart of vision's essence shown.

We chart the stars, the earth we mold,
Design the age in glints of gold,
Innovation guides our way,
From night to dawn, from dusk to day.

Community in every wall,
Spaces where our spirits call,
Rooms of warmth, streets of cheer,
Homes that hold what we hold dear.

Beyond the plans, behind the skills,
Lie dreams that raise us, hearts that fill,
Visionary architects we stand,
Creating wonders from the land.

The Wellspring of Creativity

Beneath the bounds of thought constrained,
Lies a realm, unchained, unfeigned,
A wellspring deep of endless flow,
Where seeds of inspiration grow.

Canvas blank or silence pure,
Awaits the touch, the spark, the cure,
In swirls of color, in notes that blend,
Imagination knows no end.

Threads of dreams, the needle's flight,
Patterns form in day and night,
Brush the skies with hues divine,
In every breath, creation's sign.

Whispered words or sculpted clay,
A voice, a vision finds its way,
From heart to hand, from mind to light,
Art unveils its secret might.

Boundless sea of thoughts released,
In endless forms, our souls are eased,
At the wellspring's edge, we stand awe,
Where creativity's wonders draw.

Imagination Unleashed

Unchain the thoughts that loiter bound,
Let fantasies and dreams surround,
Imagination's wings unfurled,
Take flight beyond the waking world.

In realms where dragons weave and roar,
And oceans kiss uncharted shore,
Create with wonder, passion, might,
Where shadows sing in magic's light.

Sky of purple, fields of blue,
A twilight realm, a dawn anew,
Stitch the stars in tales of gold,
A universe that we behold.

Dim the lights, let visions soar,
Through hidden doors, through ancient lore,
Unveil the realms that minds have reached,
In splendor bright, imagination's unleashed.

We dream, we craft, we find our place,
In endless forms of time and space,
In every heart, a canvas clear,
Imagination whispers near.

Paradigm Shifters

Where mind and matter meld and sway,
In realms where shadows learn to play,
We break the molds, converse with light,
New patterns forming in the night.

A spark of thought becomes a blaze,
In quantum worlds, the minds amaze,
Old dogmas tremble, walls collapse,
The future's rhythm fills the gaps.

Beyond equations, through the haze,
The seekers venture, not a phase,
With courage carved from latent dreams,
They traverse all life's vast extremes.

Chasing concepts, bending space,
Time itself can't keep its pace,
Paradigm shifters lead the way,
Crafting dawn from dusk's decay.

Ideation in Bloom

Thoughts uncoil like morning dew,
Petals open, skies anew,
In gardens lush with mental flair,
Ideas blossom, everywhere.

Pollinate the mind with stars,
Dreams escape their golden jars,
Epiphanies, like bees, alight,
On blooms that bask in twilight.

From soil of questions, stems arise,
Branching out toward curious skies,
Each ideology a bud,
Breaking through the mental mud.

Sunshine thoughts and moonlit muses,
Fertile minds produce no loses,
In the field where visions land,
Ideation takes its stand.

The Forge of Dreams

In twilight's gleam, where shadows dance,
The forge of dreams offers its chance,
To mold ambition from desire,
And set the heart's true path on fire.

From molten thoughts in fervent heat,
Aspirations find their beat,
With every hammer, every spark,
A dream is shaped, leaves its mark.

Through trials fierce and tempests wild,
Each crafted vision, undefiled,
Emerges solid, pure, and true,
A testament to what we choose.

In anvils of the mind's vast field,
Potential's ore is slowly healed,
The forge of dreams, a timeless space,
Where human spirit finds its grace.

The Horizon of Thought

Eyes cast toward the furthest edge,
Where known and unknown worlds allege,
A boundary where ideas meet,
Beyond that line, new notions greet.

With sails of wisdom, doubts unbind,
We cross the seas of curious mind,
Horizons stretch, dissolve the fears,
Each wave a window through the years.

In realms unseen, our thoughts aspire,
To touch the stars, ignite the fire,
Expand the borders of our lore,
To comprehend, explore, and more.

Horizon's lure, an endless quest,
Where intellect and dreams invest,
A journey through the cosmic weave,
The tapestry of thoughts we leave.

The Engine of Progress

In the heartbeat of the steel,
Innovation starts to reel.
Under gears and bolts confined,
Future paths we seek and find.

Driven by the need to grow,
Boundaries flex, horizons glow.
For the brave, the engine paves,
Countless dreams from endless waves.

Industry and minds entwined,
Forges strength in humankind.
Down the tracks of time, we race,
Fueled by change, we find our place.

Challenges, like ghosts in shade,
Are but steps in grand parade.
Against the weight, we do persist,
In progress, we truly exist.

From the dawn to setting sun,
Every spark a race begun.
Through each effort, bold and bright,
We embrace our endless flight.

Minds Ablaze

Thoughts combust in radiant flare,
Ideas glisten, fill the air.
In the crucible of night,
Minds ablaze, a guiding light.

Conscious worlds we intertwine,
Boundless spark, beyond define.
In this fire, we craft and weave,
Dreams so vast they scarce believe.

Contours shift within our gaze,
In the shadows, brilliance plays.
Reasoned hearts and visions clear,
Forge a future free from fear.

Every wisp of thought holds might,
In the vast and endless night.
With each ember, rivers flow,
Ignite the paths we long to know.

Flesh and spirit, bound in quest,
In this blaze, we seek our best.
To the stars our minds shall raise,
Ceaseless, endless, worlds ablaze.

Chronicles of Creativity

In the tapestry of thought,
Endless wonders to be sought.
Through the muse's dance, we see,
Chronicles of creativity.

Eager minds and restless hands,
Shape the seas and craft the lands.
From the void, we bring to air,
Stories wrought with loving care.

Colors blend and words unite,
Crafting worlds within our sight.
Every stroke and every line,
Breeds a truth almost divine.

Genius drifts on gentle breeze,
In the swirl of galaxies.
Ever-changing, bound to roam,
Weave the tales that make us home.

Inspiration's endless flame,
Calls the bold to seek acclaim.
Through our art and through our prose,
Human spirit ever grows.

Quantum Leaps

In realms unseen by naked eyes,
Microcosms mesmerize.
Particles with secrets deep,
Teach us how to take a leap.

Timeless dance of quarks and waves,
Beyond the limits, science paves.
In each heartbeat, knowledge sown,
Universe to us is shown.

Mysteries at every turn,
Make our curious minds yearn.
Tiny leaps and giant bounds,
Echo in the cosmic sounds.

Linked by threads unseen, complex,
Quantum paths our thoughts perplex.
From the vast to smallest grain,
Wisdom from this strange domain.

Expanding frontiers, great and small,
Through the quantum, we stand tall.
In the leaps we dare to take,
Wondrous futures we shall make.

Rise of the Originals

Born from shadows, pure and bold,
Their voices echo, stories unfold,
In a world that's often cold,
Untold truths now sung, retold.

With every step, unique they stand,
Casting visions over the land,
Dreams painted by their own hand,
Original spirits, truly grand.

Breaking molds with might and art,
Passion burns within their heart,
Each day marks a brand new start,
Crafting life, their finest part.

Challenges faced with fierce resolve,
In originality, they evolve,
Mysteries deep, they seek to solve,
In their hearts, the world revolve.

Stand tall, Originals, strong and free,
Your legacy shapes destiny,
In your path, we all decree,
A world where true selves can be.

Embracing the New

Horizons wide, we venture through,
Old paths fade, we seek the new,
In courage, dreams we renew,
Embracing change with a bolder view.

Unknown plains, we boldly tread,
Past fears we leave, no longer led,
New dawn rises ahead,
On hope and joy, we steadfastly fed.

In every turn, a chance to find,
Answers clear, not far behind,
Treasures hidden in the mind,
Gems of thought so rare, refined.

Clutch tight to visions bright,
In the vast expanse, take flight,
Through darkest hours, sparks ignite,
Guiding stars in the night.

Faces new, stories unfold,
From different lands, tales untold,
A tapestry, rich and bold,
In every thread, a love that holds.

Shaping Tomorrow

In dreams of youth, tomorrow lies,
With visions broad, we aim the skies,
Determined hearts, never disguise,
To change the world, future's prize.

Through trials fought, wisdom grows,
Seeds of hope, each one sows,
In unity, our power flows,
Together, a new day shows.

With hands that build and minds that dare,
Injustice bold, we do not spare,
Creating worlds where all can share,
A tomorrow bright, beyond compare.

From old constraints, we break away,
Find new paths in light of day,
In every word and deed, we say,
Innovate, enlighten, lead the way.

Shaping dreams with every stride,
In hearts of hope, we do confide,
From distant shores to countryside,
Our future's light future's guide.

The Art of Novelty

In the brush's sweep, the tale begins,
Colors blend, where time thins,
In each line, the spirit wins,
Capturing life where art within spins.

Words that dance, melodies play,
Thoughts in rhythm come to stay,
In novel forms, we find our way,
Expressing truths in a new array.

Boards are set for tales untold,
In every stroke, courage bold,
Creation's beauty, uncontrolled,
An artful journey, manifold.

Ideas bloom like morning's light,
From the shadows of the night,
In every star and every sight,
Novelty sparks pure delight.

So we craft this endless sea,
Of dreams and hopes, wild and free,
In the art of what can be,
Our hearts find creativity.

Printed in the USA
CPSIA information can be obtained
at www.ICGtesting.com
CBHW072010100824
12961CB00027B/1355